HOW TO LIVE WELL

William Perkins

Vintage Puritan Series
GLH Publishing

Originally titled *How to live, and that well: in all estates and times. Specially when helps and comforts fail.* 1601.

© GLH Publishing, 2025

Our *Vintage Puritan* Series attempts to republish classic Puritan works in a more readable format while retaining the original wording and flavor of the author's writing.

ISBN:
Paperback 978-1-64863-152-8
Epub 978-1-64863-153-5

Visit www.GLHPublishing.com to learn more about us and receive a free ebook.

CONTENTS

To the Reader 1

Treatise 3

To the Reader

Good Reader, if thou wouldst be saved by thy faith in Christ after death: thou must here live by it before death. And faith for the time of this life, hath two great uses. The first is to cut off worldly sorrows and cares. It is the common fashion of men, to multiply their cares out of measure, and thereby to make their lives most miserable. For first of all, beside necessary labours, they take up on them many needless and superfluous businesses. Secondly their manner is, to care not only for the labours to be done, but also for the event and success of their labours, that they may always prosper and never be crossed: but this care belongs to God alone. Thirdly they content not themselves; with their lot and condition, but seek by all means to increase their estate, and to make themselves rich. Lastly they exercise themselves not only in disposing of things present, but they forecast many matters in their heads, and plot the success of things to come. Now faith, when we have done the works of our callings according to the prescript of the word of God, faith (I say) makes us commend to God the blessing, success, & event thereof by prayer and affiance in his promises, not doubting but he will give us all things necessary. And if we want the blessing and success we look for, yet faith makes us to renounce our own desires, and in silence to quiet our hearts in the good pleasure of God. And thus many worldly cares are cut off.

Secondly, when a man at his wits end, knows not what in the world to do, being (as it were) plunged into a sea of miseries, faith gives direction and stays the mind. For when all temporal things fail us even to the very skin and life, faith preserves within us an affiance of the grace and mercy of God, and the hope of life everlasting. Faith shows us hidden things not to be discerned by sense and reason. Life everlasting is promised us, but we die for all that: we hear of the resurrection, but in the mean season we rot in our graves: we are pronounced blessed, but yet we are overwhelmed with infinite miseries: abundance of all things is promised, but for all this we often hunger and thirst: God promiseth to hear us and to be present with us, but he seem oft times to be deaf (as it were) at our cries. Now then comes faith, which is the substance of things hoped for, and makes us lift our minds above the whole world, to apprehend the invisible and unspeakable things of God which he hath revealed and promised unto us. These things I show more at large in this small treatise following; read it at thy leisure, use it for thy good, and see thou be a doer of them.

WILLIAM PERKINS.

Treatise

The Just Man Shall Live By His Faith.
Habakkuk 2:4

In the former chapter the Prophet complains, and expostulates the matter with God, why the Jews, the people of God, should be oppressed by the Chaldeans, the enemies of God. In the beginning of the second chapter the Lord makes answer to the Prophet, and the effect of the answer is this: They shall certainly be delivered in the time appointed, but they shall not yet be delivered. Upon this answer the Prophet might haply object on this manner: How then shall the afflicted Jews be able to live in the mean season? The Lord answers by a distinction thus; The unjust man puffs up himself with vain confidence, but the just man shall live by his faith.

For the better understanding of the words, five things are in order to be explained. The first, what is meant by the just man. *Justice* mentioned in the word is two-fold: the justice of the law, and the justice of the Gospel. The justice of the law hath in it all the points and parts of justice, and all the perfection of all parts: and it was never found in any upon earth except Adam and Christ. The justice of the Gospel, hath all the parts of true justice, but it wants the full perfection of parts: as a child hath all the parts of a man in the infancy, though it want perfection of stature and tallness. And this kind of justice is nothing else, but the conversion of a sinner, with a purpose, will, and endeavour to please God, according to all the commandments of the law. Thus was Noah, Job, Zachariah, and Elizabeth just: and thus must the just man be taken in this place for one that turns to God, and by grace endeavours to please God, according to the whole law of God in his place and calling.

The second point to be considered is, what life is here meant? As death is here two-fold, the first and the second; so is life. The first is the conjunction of the body and the soul, the second is the conjunction of the whole man with God. The first is called natural, the second spiritual or eternal life: and both are meant in this place. For Paul brings this very text to prove the justification of a sinner by faith;[1] and justification is a part of spiritual life: because it is the acceptation of a sinner to eternal life. And for this cause the Prophet says, The just man shall live, having relation not only to the time of affliction then to come, but also to eternal life.

The third point to be considered is, what is the faith here meant? And that is in justifying or saving faith; because we must live by the same faith, whereby we are saved. And faith hath his effect not only after this life, but also in this life. We must live first by it before we can be saved by it. Paul therefore in his own example expounding this text, says, "And in that I live in the flesh, I live by the faith of the son of God, who hath loved me,

---

[1] Rom. 1:17; Gal. 3:11

and given himself for me."[2]

The fourth point is the construction of the words; and that is two ways. The first is thus, *The just by faith shall live*: the words *by faith*, being joined upon the word *just*. And then the sense is this: He that is just by faith shall live or have eternal life. The second is thus; *The just, shall live by his faith*: the words *by faith*, being joined to the words *shall live*: and then the sense is this: The just while he lives in this world, he shall live by his faith. This latter construction and sense, I rather choose and embrace, because Paul, even in this sense brings this text[3] to prove that life eternal, and consequently justification comes not by working according to the law, but by believing, and he makes an exposition between *living by faith, and living by works*.

The fifth and last point to be considered is, how a man should live by faith. Because this last point is of great moment, I will spend some time in the explaining of it. That a man then may live by his faith, two things are required: the first, that faith be rightly conceived and grounded in the heart; the second, that after it is once conceived, it reign and rule in the heart. That faith may rightly be conceived, two things are required. The first is the knowledge of the word of God, for faith stands in relation to the word: and the word alone is the foundation of our faith. Hereupon the word is called the *foundation of the Prophets and Apostles*.[4] By light of natural reason we understand, that the world had a beginning and was made of God. Yet

2   Gal. 2:20

3   Gal. 3:11, 12

4   Eph. 2:20

cannot reason breed in us a certain persuasion of this point, but only the testimony of the word of God: and therefore it is said, *By faith we understand that the world was ordained by God.*[5] And this made David say, *In God I will praise his word.*[6] Furthermore, in the Word three things are to be known, *precepts* or commandment, because they teach obedience: *threatenings*, because they restrain disobedience: *promises*, because they serve to confirm us in our obedience. Again, promises are either principal or less principal. The main or principal promise is that, in which God offereth and revealeth righteousness and life everlasting by Christ. Within this promise is contained the grant of remission of our sins, of necessary patience, of the assistance of the spirit of God, and of all gifts that are inseparably joined with faith. Promises less principal are concerning deliverances in temptations, safety in dangers, health, wealth, liberty, peace, &c. And these must all be understood with an exception of the cross and correction: and they shall so far forth be accomplished as they serve for God's glory and the good of them that believe. Now all these heads and points of the word of God must be known, and that in some particular sort, that a man may live by his faith.

The second thing required for the right conceiving of faith is, after the word of God is once known, *to trust God upon his word*: yea to depend upon it, and to build up on it. This is the first and principal work of true faith: and it is called by

---

[5] Heb. 11:3

[6] Psa. 56:4

Paul *the obedience of faith*[7] and it is made the end and scope of the preaching of the Gospel: and not without cause. For this is the first and principal honour of God, to believe him upon his bare word; and thereby to make a confession of the truth of God. This the devil knew right well: and therefore the first thing that he sought to overthrow in Adam, was his faith in the word of God: and the scope of the first temptation, whereby he assaulted our Saviour Christ, was to overthrow that faith and confidence he had in his father: saying, *If thou be the son of God, command that these stones be made bread*:[8] but this thou canst not doe: therefore thou art not the son of God.

That this obedience, which we give to God by trusting his very word, may be right obedience, it must have six conditions. First of all, it must be *absolute*, for we must (as it were) shut up our own eyes, and simply without any more ado trust God upon his bare and naked word, and suffer ourselves to be lead by it. In natural things experience is first, and then faith comes afterward. And Thomas following nature desired first to feel, before he would believe. But God must be trusted, though that which he says be against reason and experience. Thus Abraham believed God *against all human hope*.[9] The second condition is, that this obedience must be *sincere*. For we must trust God's word for itself, because it is God's word; all by respects set apart. They which are as the stony ground receive God's word and rejoice in it:

7   Rom. 1:5
8   Matt. 4:3
9   Rom. 4:18

and yet afterward in time of temptation go a wry. The reason is, because they *receive the word*, and *rejoice in it*, not properly for itself, but in respect of honour, profit, or pleasure, which they look to reap thereby.[10] John the Baptist was a *burning candle*: and the Jews rejoiced in his light, only in respect of the novelty of it: and therefore the Holy Ghost says, *They rejoiced in it but for a season*.[11] The third condition is, that we must trust God not in a part, but *in his whole word*: and therefore many fail in their faith, that are content to trust him in his promises of mercy and salvation, but list not to believe him in his commandments and threats. The fourth condition is, that we must trust God in his word, *with all our hearts*, that it may take deep root and be an *ingrafted word*. It is not sufficient for us to have a taste of the good word of God, and to receive it with joy unless we thoroughly and soundly build and rely ourselves upon it. The fifth condition is, that this trusting of God must be with an *honest heart*, that is, with an heart in which there is a distinct and settled purpose not to sin, but in all things to do the will of God. The good hearers are they which receive the word *with an honest and good heart*.[12] Without this can no man possibly live by faith. He that *puts away his good conscience, makes shipwreck of his faith*.[13] It is godliness alone that hath the promises of this life and the life to come. And none can live the life of faith, but he that is a just man. After that men have made some good pro-

10 Luke 8:13
11 John 5:35
12 Luke 8:15
13 1 Tim. 1:19

ceedings, and do know the word, receive it, rejoice in it, and bring forth some fruit: if the heart for all this be *evil*, it will cause them at length *to depart from God*, by distrusting or by denying credence to his word. The sixth condition is that the obedience of faith must be *stable and constant*. The Lord saith, *my soul hath no pleasure in them that withdraw themselves*,[14] that is, which for a time believe God, and afterward pull back their foot and go back from their faith.

Seeing this is the right way to conceive faith, to know the word of God and to trust him upon the same word, all such as would live by faith, must have their hearts kindled with a desire to do the things be for named, specially to give credence to every word of God. We may not forsake God for any creature: now we forsake him, when we distrust him in his word. Again not to believe God, is very atheism. For by this means God is made a liar, and his glory and majesty is abolished. It is the greatest part of our glory to believe God: as Christ saith, *He that receives his testimony, puts to his seal, that God is true*:[15] that is, gives unto God, as it were, a testimonial of his truth, and thereto puts his hand and seal. And what greater honour can there be then this, that the creature should give testimony to the creator?

Thus much of the conceiving of faith: now follows the reign of faith. The reign of faith is, when it bears rule and sway in heart and life. For where faith is, there neither thought, will, affection, nor lust reigns, but faith alone. It reigns by two ac-

14 Heb. 10:38
15 John 3:33

tions. First of all it moves and makes us to attend on the calling of God, and yield subjection to him in all his commandments. Paul saith, that faith *establisheth the law*:[16] and one reason is because it makes us do that which the law prescribes. Again Paul saith, that his *weapons are spiritual and mighty, bringing every thought in subjection to God*.[17] Now these *mighty weapons* are the word of God preached and believed. He that is borne of God can not sin,[18] because the *seed of God* remains in him, that is, the word mingled with faith. Noah's faith made him build an ark at God's commandment:[19] after it was made, to enter into it, and not to dare to come out of it till he had warrant from God. Abraham's faith made him forsake his country and kindred at God's commandment, and go he knew not whither.[20] And that good obedience may be performed to every commandment of God, faith works two things in us, *memory and attention*. *Memory*, whereby God's word is laid up in the heart; that it may be drawn out to use when occasion shall be offered.[21] *Attention* is, when faith makes us seriously to consider and to believe that the commandment of God is a commandment not for form, but in truth, and that it does indeed pertain to us.[22] An example of both these actions of faith we have in Joseph, who, when he was tempted to folly of Po-

16 Rom. 3:31
17 2 Cor. 10:4-5
18 1 John 3:9
19 Heb. 11:7
20 Gen. 12:4
21 Psa. 119:11
22 Act. 16:14

tiphar's wife, answered, *Shall I do this wickedness, and sin against God.*[23] Mark here how his mind was filled and possessed with a thought and consideration of God's commandment.

The second action of faith whereby it reigns in the heart, is to establish and confirm them that believe in their obedience and subjection to God. And this it does, by presenting God's promises to the mind. For by means of them it worketh four actions in the heart. First of all, it makes us fly unto the true God alone, whose the promises are. Secondly, it makes us to believe that God both can and will help us according to our need. Thirdly, it makes us to hope for his help, that is, for good success in prosperity and deliverance, or some mitigation of our evils in adversity, according to the tenour of his promises. Lastly, though temporal blessings fail, it makes us still to rest on God for mercy and for life everlasting. And thus at all times it makes God to be our refuge, our castle, our rock, and tower of defence. Thus we see generally how faith reigns.

To proceed further, the just man lives a double life, namely a spiritual life and a temporal, and both of them are led by faith; as I will plainly manifest. *Spiritual life*, which is the beginning of eternal life, stands specially in four things. Reconciliation with God, peace of conscience, joy of the Holy Ghost, and newness of life. Touching reconciliation with God in Christ; it is revealed, offered, and given unto us in the main promises of the Gospel, and in the Sacraments: and it is no way in this world made ours and holden of us, but

---

23 Gen. 39:9

by our faith. And in the case of our reconciliation with God, faith hath two actions, one to receive it, the other to assure us of it.

Touching the first, faith apprehends and receives reconciliation on this manner. First of all the spirit of God works in a man a general faith of the law and the threatenings thereof, and it is called *the spirit of bondage to fear*.[24] Because it causeth in us a sight of our sins, an apprehension of God's anger, fear of due and deserved condemnation, despair of ourselves in respect of ourselves. This being done, the same spirit worketh in us another faith called *saving* or *justifying* faith, and it apprehendeth or receiveth Christ with his benefits, by certain steps and degrees, and they are specially three. For first of all upon a thorough touch and lively sense of our misery, there ariseth in the mind an earnest and serious meditation of the promise of mercy and the benefits therein offered: and it is called the opening or *piercing of the ear*.[25] Then in the second place there follows a purpose, will, desire, and in endevour to believe upon consideration of the commandment of God that bids us to believe and apply the promise to ourselves.[26] And further this will and desire shows itself by instant and serious invocation, which is nothing else but a flying from the condemning sentence of the law, to the *throne of grace* for mercy.[27] Thirdly after this, there follows in process of time, a settling and quieting of the mind touching Christ and his ben-

24 Rom. 8:15

25 Psa, 40:6

26 1 John 3:29

27 Heb. 4:16

efits upon some assurance thereof, wrought and conceived in the mind by the spirit of God. And this third degree is called an *established thought*.[28] On this manner come we by degrees to receive Christ for our full reconciliation with God. For, when upon the commandment to believe, we do in any measure believe Christ to be our Christ, he is our Christ indeed according to the tenour of the Evangelical covenant. Thus, faith apprehending Christ for our reconciliation with God, becomes a *victorious conquerour* and prevails against the Law, Satan, hell, death, condemnation, and all our spiritual enemies: and thus every believer is above the Law, sin, hell, death, even in this life.

The second action of faith in the case of our reconciliation with God, is to certify and assure us in conscience thereof: and that is done by a practical syllogism, which faith frames in the mind on this manner:

> *He that believes the Gospel, shall have all the benefits and blessing of God promised therein.*
> *But I believe the Gospel, and I believe in Christ:*
> *Therefore the benefits promised therein are mine.*

The *major* or first part of this reason, is the voice of the Gospel: the *minor* or the second part is the voice of the believing heart, which subjecteth itself in will and affection to the commandment which bids us believe in Christ: and this is the act of special faith. And we may not think that this voice of the believing heart is a false alarm. For he that truly believes hath his mind and conscience supernaturally in lightened to discernment that he

---

[28] Isa. 26:3

believes. The third part, or the conclusion is the foundation of all our joy and spiritual comfort. For it contains in it the chiefest certainty of our adoption and salvation that can be had in this life, namely the certainty of faith, whence follows in a lower degree in the second place, the certainty that is by works. And thus does faith certify all such as truly believe that they are the children of God.

Out of the former conclusion, or out of the certainty which is by faith, follows a full and lively certainty of the doctrine of the Gospel, worthy [of] consideration on this manner. There is a threefold certainty: the first is certainty of reason or of general faith, when a man by force of argument is convicted of the certainty of the doctrine of the Bible. This may be in the wicked and ungodly without faith in Christ. After this, in the elect by a more special work of God's spirit, follows a faith in Christ, and the certainty of justifying or special faith expressed in the conclusion of the former syllogism. Thirdly, after this certainty of special faith follows another experimental certainty of the truth of the Bible, which also faith concludes on this manner:

That doctrine which assures us to be God's children is certainly of God.
But the doctrine of the Gospel, believed or mingled with our faith, assures us to be God's children.
Therefore it is of God.

The *major* is granted of all: the *minor* is in effect the conclusion of the former syllogism, and it is known by an experience of that spiritual comfort which the godly feel in their hearts. The conclusion sets down the certainty of the Bible upon a further ground, then any wit or learning of man can attain unto without the spirit of grace, namely upon an inward assurance of our reconciliation with God. Of this certainty our Saviour Christ speaks notably, *If any man will doe my Father's will*, that is, believe it, and subject himself to it, *he shall know* [namely, by that comfort which he shall feel upon his subjection] *of the doctrine, whether it be of God, or whether I speak of myself.*[29] And Paul says, *that the spiritual man*, that is, one regenerate by the spirit of God, *judgeth all things.*[30] Hence it follows, that such as desire to be settled for their religion, and such as desire to be good and profitable students in divinity, must first of all humble themselves and endeavour in their hearts truly to believe in Christ. Because hence flows the best experience of the certainty and consequently of the unspeakable excellency of the Bible.

Thus, then we see how we are to receive, hold, and enjoy our reconciliation with God in Christ, by no other thing within us, but by means of our faith alone. And therefor we must have special care, that we may by the use of God's means attain to a lively faith. And for this cause we must do two things: first we are to labour to be convicted in conscience of the certainty of the word. This done, we must then subject our wills to the commandment of God that bid us believe in Christ: we must bewail our unbelief: we must strive against the same, and pray unto God to confirm and increase our faith, by establishing our hearts in his love.

29 John 7:17
30 1 Cor. 2:15

The second part of spiritual life is *peace of conscience*, which is nothing else but a constant and stable tranquility of mind, when the conscience does not accuse, but excuse: and when neither hell, death, condemnation, nor any danger is feared overmuch. This peace was in David, when he said, *I laid me down and slept and rose again*,[31] in the middest of manifold dangers. This peace is of great excellency, for it is *the peace of God*:[32] it is one part of *the kingdom of God*:[33] it passeth all understanding: it is in stead of a guard to keep our hearts and minds in Christ. Now this excellent peace springs out of our faith, whereby we believe our reconciliation with God. *Being justified by faith we have peace with God*.[34] *Trust in the Lord and ye shall be secure*.[35] Yea, as our faith is, so is our peace: lively faith, lively peace: constant faith, constant peace: faith in life, peace in life: faith in death, peace in death: so as we may say with Simeon; *Lord, now lettest thou thy servant depart in peace*.[36]

The third part of spiritual life is, the *joy of the Holy Ghost*:[37] and that is to rejoice in God because he is our God, and in Christ because he is our Christ. And this kind of joy is not taken from us or abated in afflictions, but rather increased. *We rejoice in tribulations*.[38] And, *Ye endured the spoiling of*

31 Psa. 3:5
32 Phil. 4:7
33 Rom. 14:17
34 Rom. 5:1
35 2 Chron. 20:20
36 Luke 2:29
37 Phil. 3:1
38 Rom. 5:3

your goods with joy.[39] Now, our faith in the promise of life is the mother and breeder of this joy, which a riseth of that happy and blessed conclusion that faith frames in the mind; I believe: therefore the blessings of God promised in the Gospel, are mine. Thus saith Saint Peter, *Believing ye rejoice with joy unspeakable and glorious.*[40] Again the continuance and in crease of our faith, is the increase of this joy.

The last part of spiritual life is *newness of life* and conversation, whereby we are born anew and made new creatures: not because the substance of body and soul is changed, but because the image of God is restored. Now this change both for the whole and for the parts thereof is by faith. Touching the whole: men as they are new creatures have their beginning from the word of promise, or from Christ crucified who is propounded in the promise, and that as the said word, or Christ is apprehended by faith. *Your hearts being purified by faith.*[41] *He which hath this hope, purifieth himself.*[42] *Your souls are purified in obeying the truth.*[43] And again, *being born anew of the immortal seed of the word.*

The parts of newness of life are specially three. True wisdom, good affections, and good works. True wisdom is to advise of good things, and to use good means for the execution thereof. This wisdom ariseth of our faith in the word of God. David says, *He was wiser than his teachers, and wiser*

---

39 Heb. 10:34

40 1 Pet. 1:8

41 Acts 15:9

42 1 John 3:3

43 1 Pet. 1:22

than the ancient:[44] and he renders the cause thereof from the work of his faith; *For thy testimonies are ever with me, and they are my meditation.* Out of the same fountain spring all good affections. The love whereby we love God, comes of our faith, believing the love wherewith God loveth us. The persuasion of the forgiveness of many sins in the woman that washed Christ's feet with her tears, caused her to show much love to Christ.[45] Godly sorrow, when the heart is grieved properly for the offence of God, ariseth of faith apprehending and believing the mercy of God in Christ. And in every good work, there is a threefold action of faith required. First there is required an act of general faith, which is to believe that the work to be done in his kind pleaseth God. *Whatsoever is not of faith is sin.*[46] The second is an act of justifying faith, which is to purge the heart, and to cause it to bring forth the good work to be done. *I believed, therefore I spoke.*[47] The third is also an act of justifying faith, and that is when the work is done, to apprehend Christ who by his merit is to cover the defect of the work: because no work of ours can please God without remission of sin.

Thus newness of life with all the parts thereof, hath his offspring of our faith. Yea after that a man is once made a new creature, faith gives him his life and sense: faith is the eye of the mind whereby we behold Christ in the word and sacraments. By

44 Psa. 119:98, 99
45 Luke 7:47
46 Rom. 14:23
47 Psa. 116:10

this faith *Abraham saw the day of Christ and rejoiced.*[48] With this eye we may sufficiently behold Christ; and bodily sight in this case is not necessary for the time of this life: therefore Christ saith, *Blessed are they which have not seen and have believed.*[49] Again, faith is the hand of the soul, whereby we lay hold on Christ and receive him with all his benefits. It is the mouth of the heart, whereby we feed on Christ, eating his body and drinking his blood to eternal life. It is the feet of the soul, that makes us *walk with God.*[50] Lastly, it is a means to bring us into familiarity with God. For it is an ear whereby we hear God speak to us in his word; and it is as it were the tongue of the soul, whereby we speak to God by invocation of his holy name.

To go yet further, spiritual life is most of all manifest in afflictions and temptations, in the bearing where of faith reigns: and that by a threefold action. First of all, it makes us to depend on God's promises and to trust God without limitation. For it does not limit God to any set time of deliverance, but leaves all to God. *He that believes, does not make hast.*[51] Daniel waited 70 years for deliverance out of captivity in Babylon, and then finding the time of deliverance to be at hand, he prayed to God for the same.[52] Again, faith does not limit God to any means of deliverance. God made promise to Abraham of a blessed seed. For the verifying of this promise he gave him Isaac in his old

48 John 8:56
49 John 20:29
50 Gen. 5:22
51 Isa. 28:16
52 Dan. 9:10

age. This done, he commands him to offer his only son in sacrifice. A grievous cross: for by this means all hope is cut off, touching the promised seed. Yet by faith Abraham still believes the promise, and that in the very offering of his son. Lastly, faith does not limit God for the measure of affliction. Job saith, *He will trust in God though he kill him*.[53] It was a grievous affliction for David to be driven out of his kingdom by his own son, yet mark what he saith in the flight: *If he say, I have no delight in thee, behold here I am, let him do unto me as shall seem good in his eyes*.[54] The second action of faith is to make us believe the promises of God when we feel the contrary and in one contrary to believe an other. When we feel our own sins, it makes us believe our justification: when we feel our wretchedness and misery, it makes us believe our happiness: when we feel nothing but death, it makes us believe our eternal salvation: when we apprehend God's anger and feel him to be our enemy, it makes us to apprehend his mercy and to believe his fatherly kindness. When Christ was forsaken of God, he even then by his faith believes God to be his God. The third action of faith in afflictions, is to assure us of God's presence, and to behold him with the eyes of faith. Thus David says, *I have set the Lord all ways before me: for he is at my right hand*.[55] Moses left Egypt and feared not the wrath of the king *because he saw him that was invisible*.[56] When the servant of Elisha feared over much the

---

53 Job 13:15

54 2 Sam. 15:26

55 Psa. 16:8

56 Heb. 11:27

host of the king of Syria that compassed the town of Dothan, the Prophet prays to God for him that his eyes might be opened, to see the fiery chariots of the angels of God protecting him:[57] and we likewise are to pray to God, that the eyes of our minds may be opened to believe and to acknowledge the same or the like protection. And thus are men to live by faith in the midst of their afflictions.

By this which hath been said, we are admonished first of all to acquaint ourselves with the promises of God, as they are recorded in the books of the Prophets and Apostles: secondly at all times to build upon them by our faith, and not to suffer ourselves to be drawn from them, though all temporal blessings of God fail us, yea health and life itself. This is to arm ourselves with a shield against all the fiery darts of the devil,[58] and to put on a *breast-plate* that will save the heart and life,[59] though otherwise in temptations we be grievously maimed and foiled.

Thus much of spiritual life. That our temporal life is lead by faith, I make it thus manifest. Temporal life is preserved and maintained by an honest calling: every calling hath his labour and work: and the labour of all callings hath misery and trouble for his companion and fellow; and in all these faith reigns and bears the sway in them that believe.

For the first, that is for the choosing and holding of our callings with good conscience, there is required a double use of faith. For we must have

[57] 2 Kings 6:15

[58] Eph. 6:16

[59] 2 Thess. 5:8

a faith, whereby we must be assured that our callings are good and lawful in themselves: as Paul saith, *Whatsoever is not of faith is sin*.[60] For the settling of this faith, this rule must be remembered, that offices and callings which serve to preserve the good estate of any family, Church, or commonwealth, are lawful and of God: because these are estates ordained of God, and established in the commandment of the moral law, specially in the first, fifth, and sixth commandments. Again, faith is required, whereby every man must believe that the calling in which he is; is the particular calling in which God will be served of him. For unless the conscience be settled in this, no good work can be done in any calling. And for the better establishing of the conscience, another rule must be remembered, That they which are furnished with gifts for their callings, namely aptness and willingness, and are thereunto called or set apart by men whom it concerns to call, are indeed called of God. Thus the elders of Ephesus, having gifts to feed, and being not called of God immediately, but by men, are said to be *made overseers by the Holy Ghost*. And Paul saith, that God committed not only to himself but also to Timothy the ministry of reconciliation:[61] and yet was Timothy not called immediately of God, but by men.[62] And thus, in all other offices and conditions of life, he that hath gifts fit for his place, and is in good manner called thereto by them whose duty it is to call, may assure himself, that he is called of God. And from this double

60 Rom. 14:23

61 2 Cor. 5:18

62 1 Tim. 4:14

faith and persuasion, that our calling is lawful in itself, and lawful or pleasing God in respect of us, ariseth an assurance of the presence of God, and of his protection, when we walk in the duties of our callings.

In the labour and work of our calling there is required a double action of faith. The first is to order our labours, that they be done in good manner, that is, in obedience, and to good ends, that is, to God's glory, and to the good of men with whom we live. In this respect is *Noah said to build an Ark by faith*,[63] and good princes to order their common wealths, and in way of protection to make war with their enemies: and thus must every man of every office, calling, trade, occupation, do his duty by faith.[64] The second action of faith is in our daily labours to restrain and moderate our care. Men commonly take upon them a double care; one is to do the works and labours of their callings; the other is to procure a blessing and good success to their foresaid labours. But faith in God's word where it reigns, it stirs up the hearts of men only to the first care, which is in the performance of their pain full labours and duties, and it restrains them from the second, causing them to leave it to God. For when men have done the duty that appertains unto them, then faith makes them without any more ado, to wait for a blessing on God. To this purpose the Holy Ghost saith, *Cast thy burden on the Lord, and he shall nourish thee.*[65] Again, *Be nothing careful, but in all things let your requests*

63 Heb. 11:7

64 Heb. 11:33, 34

65 Psa. 55:22

be showed unto God in prayer and supplication with thanksgiving:⁶⁶ and *Cast your care on God*.⁶⁷ Now this faith, whereby we depend on God for the success of our labours, hath an infallible ground, namely, that God best knows our wants, and he will give unto us all things which he in his wisdom knows to be necessary. Christ saith, *Your heavenly father knoweth that you have need of these things, that is, food and raiment*.⁶⁸ Again, *He careth for you*:⁶⁹ and, *Nothing shall be wanting unto them that fear God*.⁷⁰ If men would by faith build on these promises, they should not need like drudges of the world to toil and spend themselves, and the best part of their days in worldly cares, as they do: for they should have a greater blessing of God with less care, if they would trust him: and they should have far more time then they have to care for heaven and heavenly things.

Thirdly and lastly, every calling since the fall of Adam hath misery and affliction to be his companion. And for the quiet bearing of the miseries of every calling, faith is of great moment. For it works patience by persuading and settling our minds in two things: the first, that God is well pleased with us, and that we are reconciled to God in Christ: the second, that all our miseries shall in the end turn to our good and everlasting salvation. And where these two persuasions take place, there is conten-

---

66   Phil. 4:6

67   1 Pet. 5:7

68   Matt. 6:31

69   1 Pet. 5:7

70   Psa. 34:9

tation[71] in any estate.

Thus much for the meaning of the text: now follows the use. The first and principal use concerns the information of our judgment, in the main point of our salvation. For hence Paul hath taught us to gather, that a sinner is justified before God by his faith, without the works of the law. And he disputes on this manner: *If a sinner be justified by faith, he is not justified by the law: but a sinner is justified by faith, therefor he is not justified by the law.*[72] The conclusion is propounded in the eleventh verse of the 3rd chapter to the Galatians. The major is confirmed in the 12th verse by the divers manner of justifying: *The law* (saith Paul) *justifieth by doing, not by believing: and faith justifieth not by doing, but by believing.* The minor is confirmed in the 11th verse by the testimony of the prophet Habakkuk: *The just shall live by his faith.*[73] And whereas the Papists of our time say that Paul in this argument disputes only against such works of the law as are done by nature, but not by grace: they ere and are deceived. For he opposeth not works of nature and works of grace, but works and faith doing and believing: and the Prophet says very plainly, and mark it; that the just man, who is a doer of the works of grace, is justified and lives not by his works, but by his faith. Again, where they make a double justification; one whereby a sinner is made a just man, the other whereby a just man is made more just: and teach that the first is by faith without works, and the second by faith

71 Contentment

72 Gal. 3:11, 12

73 Hab. 2:4

and works, they ere likewise. For not only a sinner unconverted, but the just man stands just, and is still justified by his faith without his works. Paul, when he alleged this text, knew but of one justification, whether we respect the beginning or the continuance and the accomplishment thereof.

Secondly, hence may be learned the right way of reformation of our lives. In this reformation two things are required: an *examination* and a *change*. If we examine our lives by this text, we shall find two main faults and aberrations in the lives of men. The first is, that they reject and put away the rule of direction that serves for the ordering of their lives. And this they do, when they do not believe and trust God in his word. And we may not think, that this our unbelief is a small matter: because it is a mother sin of all other sins: and it is the principal law of the kingdom of darkness, not to believe God. Hereupon our enemy Satan endeavoured by all means to imprint this lesson of unbelief in the minds of our first parents: and having effected his purpose, he ever since endeavoured to make this sin to reign in the lives of men. It reigns commonly by seven especial fruits or sins.

The first is *Atheism*, when men deny God and his word. *Atheism* hath two parts: Epicurism and Temporising. Epicurism is when men contemning God's commandments, threatenings, promises, care for nothing but meat, drink, and pleasures. Temporising is when men embrace religion so far forth as they are forced by laws and times, and no otherwise. These are the common sins of our days.

The second fruit is *Heresy*, and that is, when men distrust God in some article of faith. This fruit abounds in this last age of the world: because in these times the devil hath revived the heresies of the former ages.

The third fruit is *Apostasy*, and that is when men change their faith and religion. And this change is made, when the evil heart of unbelief causeth them to depart from the living God.[74] This hath been the fault of the people of this land in the days of persecution.

The fourth fruit is *Hypocrisy*, which is to make a show and pretence of faith, and to want the power of it in honest and godly conversation: or again, hypocrisy is nothing else but the unbelief of the heart covered over with the false appearance of faith. And it is the common sin of these times, in which a formal or ceremonial faith and ceremonial repentance bear a great sway. For men make the highest degree of profession that can be, when they come to the Lord's table: and yet afterward take to themselves liberty to live and do as they list.

The fifth fruit is *Carnal Security*, when men upon contempt of the judgments of God, and threatenings of his word, go on still in their sins, flattering and soothing themselves. Thus the son's in-law of Lot,[75] when they heard of the destruction of Sodom, esteemed it but as a mockery. Thus did the Jews make a league with hell and death, and said with themselves that the scourges of God should not come at them.[76] And in this last age of the world, men shall wholly addict themselves

---

74 Heb. 3:12

75 Gen. 19:14

76 Isa. 28:15

to pleasures and profits, thinking nothing of any judgment of God, till vengeance befall them.

The sixth is *Willful Ignorance* of the will and word of God. For the devil blinds the minds of unbelievers, that the light of the Gospel shine not unto them.[77] This is the fault of our common people, who commonly hold an opinion, that it belongs not to them to know the word of God: because they are not learned (as they say:) or because they have other business to think on.

The last fruit is *Worldliness*, and that is when men mind nothing but worldly matters. And this comes of the want of faith in the providence of God.[78] These are the principal fruits of unbelief, whereby it may easily be discerned and dis cried where it is. And if any man think himself to have a fullness and perfection of faith, as many do; even this one thing is a sufficient argument of his unbelief. For it is the first step to faith, to see in ourselves the want of faith.

The second main aberration in the lives of men is, that they set up false rules to order their lives by: and they are four. The first is the *light of natural reason*. For many are of opinion, that it is sufficient to the pleasing of God, if they live civilly, that is, do justice to every man, and live peaceably, hurting none. This is the blind divinity of the world, that if they carry themselves thus and thus, whatsoever their sins be, God will hold them excused. But they are far wide: for in a life acceptable to God, faith is required; the light of reason will not serve the turn. Paul saith, *The wisdom of the natu-*

---

77   2 Cor. 4:4

78   Matt. 6:30

ral man is enmity to God;[79] *and he cannot discern the things of God.*[80] The Pharisees had civil justice and goodness: yet says Christ, *except your justice exceed theirs, ye cannot enter into the kingdom of heaven.*[81]

The second false rule is *sense*, that is, seeing and feeling: by this men commonly live. If we enjoy the good blessings of God, health, wealth, liberty, peace, honour, good report, then we can trust God: but if he with draw his blessings and present himself to us with an empty hand, we trust him no longer, nay we murmur and despair, and without fear of God, use any unlawful means to relieve ourselves. Though we have his precious word, yet do we not trust him upon his bare and naked word, unless withal he lay down unto us some good pawn, and make us to feel and enjoy his good blessings. Again, if any man, that is our friend, make promise of help or deliverance in any danger, we rest content and find ourselves much eased thereby: and yet the promises made by God in his word of help and deliverance, though they be often read unto us, and often urged, breed not the like contentation.[82] He that on his death-bed hath commended his children to some trusty friend, departs more quieted in mind, then if he had commended them without help of friend to God their best father. A man upon good security lends to an other, an 100 pounds hoping for the principal with the increase at the year's end: yet dare he not scarce deliver an 100 pence to the poor

79 Rom. 8:7

80 1 Cor. 2:14

81 Matt. 5:20

82 Contentment

members of Christ, upon the promise and bond of God himself, who saith, *He that gives to the poor, lends to the Lord*,[83] and he will return the said gifts with a blessing. Now all this comes to pass, because men rather trust them whom they see, than God whom they never saw. Moreover it is a property of them that do indeed believe, to judge their estate by feeling: but herein they deceive themselves. For we must live by faith and not by feeling: and feeling is often deceitful. Because such as finally fall away from God may have a feeling, or taste of the good word of God, and of the powers of the life to come.[84]

The third rule is *false faith*, which is without or against the word. Thus the Turk lives by his false faith; the Jew by his; the Papist by his, for he believes as well the traditions of men, as the word of God, and he puts his trust not only in God, but also in the creatures, namely saints and angels. Thus also do magicians, sorcerers, witches, enchanters, whatsoever they do, by a satanical faith in that covenant which they have made with the devil. And such persons ask counsel of witches and wizards, called cunning men and women; help themselves only by their false faith. For when they use charms or spells, or like satanical ceremonies, they commonly find success and are helped of the evils that betide[85] them. And that comes to pass on this manner. In the use of the foresaid ceremonies prescribed and delivered by witches, they have a blind and erroneous faith: upon their faith follows

83 Prov. 19:17

84 Heb. 6:4

85 "Happen to"

a satanical operation in effecting of the care desired. For charms or spells being but words have no virtue in them to ease or help man or beast, either by creation or by any ordinance of God in his word: and therefore the effect they have, is by the power of the devil upon mans faith. Let our common people think on this, who though they much boast of their faith in Christ, yet when they are in any extremity or danger, very commonly practice this satanical faith.

The last false rule is, the *lust of the heart*: and by this rule do most men square their lives. The lust that commonly rules is threefold: lust concerning bodily pleasure, lust of worldly wealth, lust of honour, as St. John saith, *Whatsoever is in the world, is the lust of the flesh, the lust of the eye, and the pride of life.*[86]

Thus much of the examination; now follows the change. That we may change our lives in respect of unbelief, four things are required. The first is, that we must acknowledge and bewail our unbelief with the manifold fruits thereof. And we have good cause to do so. For by unbelief the devil erects his kingdom in men's hearts, and works his pleasure in us and upon us.[87] Secondly unbelief corrupts and defiles all our actions what soever, though otherwise they be good and lawful in themselves. Paul says, that *to unbelievers all things are unclean, yea their minds and consciences are defiled.*[88] Thirdly unbelief deprives us of the good blessings of God which otherwise we might en-

86 1 John 2:16
87 Eph. 2:2
88 Tit. 1:15

joy. *If ye believe not, ye shall not be established*, saith the Prophet.[89] In Capernaum Christ could do no great wonders by reason of their unbelief.[90] Lastly unbelief plucks down up on men the plagues and judgments of God. Moses and Aaron were barred the land of Canaan for their unbelief.[91] A certain prince was trodden to death in the gates of Samaria, because he would not believe the word of the Lord by the mouth of Elisha.[92] Zachariah was dumb for a time because he would not believe the message of the angel. Many at this day, when the judgments of God lie heavy on them, say presently they are forespoken,[93] and they cry out on this or that suspected witch. But such persons are often deceived. For the great witch that does them all the hurt, is the unbelief of their hearts whereby they distrust God in his word: and this sin alone, if there were no witches in the world, is sufficient alone to provoke God to plague and punish us sundry ways, and that grievously. Therefore let us with bitterness of heart bewail our unbelief: and the rather, because it is a step to faith to acknowledge the want of faith.

The second thing to be done, is to make examination whether we be in conscience convicted of the certainty of the word or no. If we be not, we must labour to be convinced. Because that natural atheism, whereby we doubt whether the books of the Prophets and Apostles be the word of God or

89 Isa. 7:9

90 Mark 6:5

91 Num. 20:12

92 2 Kings 7:12-17

93 to predict, foresee

no, hinders the certainty of faith. For the settling of the conscience in this point, these arguments may be used. The first, it is a principle in nature that there is a God: if there be a God, nature can say he is to be worshiped: if he be to be worshiped, he hath revealed himself and his will to man, for otherwise he cannot be worshiped. And this revelation is to be found in the writings of the Prophets and Apostles, and in no other writings of men: because we find the doctrine of Scriptures to be agreeable to the very nature and majesty of God, and so is no other doctrine or learning whatsoever. For it is the most ancient, and all other religions come far short of it. It is one and the same, evermore consenting with itself, without change or alteration. The Apostles agree with the Prophets: the Prophets with Moses: and all with the first revelation made at the creation. Again, it discovers and reveals the secret thoughts of men, that no art or learning can discover: and this argues that it was penned by him who is the searcher of all hearts.[94]

The second argument is a wonderful *evidence of the truth*, not to be found in any other writings in the world. This evidence stands specially in eight things. The first is, that the writers of Scriptures fully and plainly set down their own faults,[95] yea their chiefest faults, not sparing to shame themselves in man's reason: and this argues, that in writing they were guided by the spirit of truth. The second is, that the books of Scriptures contain many mysteries above the reach of man's reason,

94 Psa. 10:6, 11, 13, 14; Luke 8:11, 12; Rev. 18:7; 1 Cor. 2:14; Matt. 12:14; Psa. 7:8; Isa. 8:15; Num. 20:12; Psa. 51; 119:11; 73:12, 13; 1 Tim. 1:13

95 Eccl. 9

yet not against reason: because we may discern a truth in them, and that by grounds and principles of reason. The third, that the speeches of Scripture aim not at by-respects, but simply and absolutely give and ascribe all glory to God alone. The fourth is, that the Scriptures contain full and perfect doctrine for the pacifying, settling, and directing of the conscience in all things. The fifth is, the holiness and purity of the law of Moses, in that it accuseth and condemneth all men of sin, and prescribeth perfect righteousness. Herein it surpasseth the laws of all countries, commonwealths, kingdoms whatsoever. The sixth is the wisdom that appears in the policy or government of the commonwealth of the Jews set down by Moses. The seventh is a reconciliation of justice and mercy propounded in the Gospel. For in Christ justice and mercy meet, and justice after a sort gives place to mercy. The eight thing wherein this evidence of truth appears, is the consent of Scripture with itself: for doctrine agrees with history, and every part with every part. This manifold evidence of truth shows that Scripture is from the God of truth. If any say, that they find no such evidence in Scripture, I answer it is their own fault: for if they would seriously read the Scriptures with prayer to God, it would appear.

The third argument is the efficacy of the word: which appears on this manner. God's word is flat contrary to the nature and corrupt disposition of man: and yet for all this, when, being preached, it convinceth and condemneth men of sin; it turneth and converteth them to itself, and causeth them to live and die in the love and obedience thereof.[96] This could it never do, unless it were of divine operation.

The fourth argument is, that the Prophets and Apostles wrought miracles for the ratifying and confirming of their doctrine. Now these miracles surpass the strength of nature, and were immediately from God: and therefor the doctrine thereby confirmed, was also of God.

The fifth and last is that the writings of the Prophets and Apostles contain many prophecies or predictions of things to come, that none could foresee or foretell, but God. The name of Josiah and his doings are foretold 330 years before he his birth.[97] Cyrus and his doings are mentioned more than a 100 years before was born:[98] now these and the like prophecies argue that the whole doctrine is of God. By these and like arguments, are all that inwardly doubt of the word of God, to settle and establish their consciences.

This done, then follows the third point, and that is, that we must search and inquire what is the substance and scope of the word of God. The scope of the whole Bible is Christ with his benefits, and he is revealed, propounded, and offered unto us in the main promise of the word: the tenour where of is, that God will give remission of sins and life everlasting to such as will believe in Christ.[99] To this main promise, God hath added a main commandment, which bids us to believe

---

96   Heb. 4:12; 2 Cor. 10:5

97   1 Kings 13:2

98   Isa. 44-66

99   1 John 3:23

the said promise, or to apply Christ with his benefits unto ourselves. Now then our third duty is to subject our hearts and wills to this commandment that bids us believe in Christ. This is the subjection of faith, of which two things must be observed. One is that this is the first subjection that we can give to God, to trust him up on his promise for the pardon of our sins, and for life eternal. And from this subjection of faith ariseth our subjection to the whole word. In Christ are all the promises of God, *yea* and *amen*:[100] the law and the obedience of all the commandments thereof is established by faith: without Christ no good thing can be done. The second point is, that this subjection is easy in respect of that subjection which the law requires. The perfect obedience of the law is impossible to all men except Christ, yea to such as are borne anew of the Holy Ghost, though for the time of this life, they desire it never so earnestly. Yet faith in Christ and repentance is so far forth possible to all that will and desire it, that whosoever does seriously but will to believe and be converted, does indeed believe and is converted, and does please God, and shall not perish eternally; although the beginning of this faith and conversion be weak, so it be in truth and not counterfeit. *If ye will and obey, ye shall eat the good things of the land.*[101] *Your heavenly father giveth the Holy Ghost to them that desire him.*[102] *My yoke is easy and my burden light.*[103] Therefore let us try ourselves whether we have a will to subject

[100] 2 Cor. 1:20

[101] Isa. 1:19

[102] Luke 11:13

[103] Matt. 11:30

ourselves to the word of God, that bids us believe in Christ. Neverthless we may not think that this will to believe is in our power. For it is by the special mercy of God stirred up in the hearts of the elect, by the operation of the Holy Ghost.

The fourth and last thing in this change is, that faith in Christ, or in the word believed, must reign and rule in the heart: bringing the whole man in subjection to the whole word of God. And this faith in Christ does: because when it is once settled in the heart, it works in us a full and settled faith of every part of the word of God; namely of his precepts and of his threats. Here then our duty is to subject ourselves by means of our faith to the whole word: and to suffer nothing within us but it alone to bear sway. This is the will of God; *let the word of God dwell in you plentifully*.[104] The good ground yields itself and gives place, that the seed may take deep root. It is a blessed thing to have the kingdom of God erected in our hearts: now this kingdom is erected, when the word of God keeps all the powers of body and soul in subjection. And when our faith in Christ brings our thoughts, affections, words, deeds, sufferings in subjection to the word of God, then we live by faith.

The third use followeth: in that we are to live by our faith, we are taught to seek for knowledge of the will and word of God, and daily to increase in the same knowledge; specially to acquaint ourselves with the commandments of God that concern us, with his promises, and threatenings. For faith is the life of our souls, and the word is the life of faith: because it is first kindled and afterward

---

104 Col. 3:16

confirmed by the hearing of God's word. Again, the word moderates our faith, that we believe not more then we should, or come short in believing. The word therefore that serves thus to limit our faith, must be known in his several heads and points.

Fourthly, hence we learn how we are to carry ourselves in greatest dangers, as in the time of plague and pestilence, in the time of famine, in the time of war and bloodshed, in the time of our last and deadly sickness. We have then need of great help: and the only way is then to stay ourselves and establish our hearts by our faith on God's promises. It is the very scope of this text to teach this one point of doctrine to the Jews, being now oppressed by the Babylonians. David in danger, and Christ in the time of his passion, by their faith commend their spirits into the hands of God. Of the martyrs and saints of God, some were by their faith imprisoned, some racked, some stoned.[105] Faith in perilous times is of great use. First, when a man is half dead, it quickens and puts life in him, as David saith, *Remember the promise made to thy servant, wherein thou hast caused me to trust: it is my comfort in my trouble: for thy promise hath quickened me.*[106] Understand here the promise as it was tempered and mingled with his faith. Again, faith in the times of danger does as it were sense and compass us with the promises of God. This may be gathered by the opposition that is between these words and the former. *The unjust man puffs up himself*; saith the Prophet, or builds towers of

[105] Heb. 11:37

[106] Psa. 119:49

defence to himself. But the just man only believes; and that shall be to him instead of all the towers in the world. For it brings us under the presence, wing, and protection of God: it makes him to be our safeguard and tower of defence. This doctrine is to be thought on the rather; because, though we now enjoy peace and other blessings of God, yet our common sins and especially our unbelief, calls down for the great and grievous judgments of God.

Moreover, hence we are taught that every man must have a faith of his own, *The just man shall live by his* OWN *faith*, says the Prophet. And good reason, for every man is a creature of God and must do his homage to God by believing in him: and because every man hath need of Christ for himself: therefore must every one have a faith of his own to lay hold on Christ. It may be objected, that some time the faith of others hath saved men. *When Christ saw their faith, he said to the sick of the palsy, Thy sins are forgiven thee.*[107] And, *The prayer of faith shall save the sick.*[108] I answer, that the faith of one man may be a means to procure health of body and other temporal blessings, yea faith unto others; yet cannot any man receive pardon of sins, and eternal life but for himself. Therefore when it is said in the first place, *When he saw their faith*, the faith of the palsy man must not be excluded but included: and the place of James speaks only of the bodily health.

Again, it may be alleged, that seeing we are justified by the justice of another, namely of Christ:

---

107 Mark 2:5

108 Jam. 5:16

we may also be justified and saved by the faith of another. I answer, that the reason is not alike, because the obedience of Christ is both his and ours: his, because it is in him: ours, because it is applied unto us by God, and received by our faith: and the like cannot be said of the faith of any other man.

Thirdly, it may be alleged, that infants have no faith of their own. I answer, there be three opinions touching infant's faith. The first, that infants have actual faith wrought in them by the Holy Ghost, because it is said, *Whatsoever offendeth one of these little ones that believes in me.*[109] But this opinion seems to be an untruth: because faith presupposeth understanding and knowledge, which infants want. Again, if infants received to believe when they are young, they would, no doubt, show it when they come to be of years: but faith they show none, unless they attain unto it afterward by diligent teaching and instruction. And the place in Matthew may be understood of men of years, who if they have contrite and humbled hearts, are little ones believing in Christ. Again, children after some years by good education and instruction, may attain to some knowledge and consequently to faith. Thus Timothy was brought up in the Scripture of a child. The second opinion is, that all places of Scripture entreating of faith are to be understood of men of years, and that children are saved by some other unknown and unspeakable way without faith. I somewhat doubt of this; because it is said, *Whosoever believeth not is already condemned.*[110] Again, *Without faith it is impossible*

---

[109] Matt. 18:6

[110] John 3:18

to please God.[111] The third opinion is, that children have faith after a sort: because the parents according to the tenour of the covenant, *I will be thy God, and the God of thy seed,*[112] believe for themselves and their children; and therefore their faith is not only theirs but also the faith of their children. Hence it is that the Scripture saith, *If the root be holy, the branches are holy;*[113] and, *If ye believe, your children are holy.*[114] According to human law, the father and his heirs are but one person, the father covenanting for himself and his children: what then should hinder, that the father might not believe for his child, and the child by the parents faith have title to the covenant, and the benefits thereof. It is alleged, that by this means children shall be born believers, and so be conceived and borne without original sin.[115] I answer, believing parents sustain two persons: one, whereby they are men; and thus they bring forth children having man's nature with all the corruptions of nature. The other, as they are holy men and believers; and thus they bring forth infants that are not so much their children as the children of God. And infants are God's children not by virtue of their birth, but by means of parent's faith, which entitles them to all the blessings of the covenant. Children proportionally sustain a double person; if they be considered in and by themselves, they are conceived and born in original sin. If they be considered as they are

111 Heb. 11:6

112 Gen. 17:7

113 Rom. 11:16

114 1 Cor. 7:14

115 Bellar. lib. 1 de bapt. cap. 4

holy and believe by the faith which is both theirs and their parents faith, and consequently have by this means title to Christ and his benefits; original sin is cove red and remitted. If it be said, that by this means all children of believing parents are the children of God; I answer, that we must presume that they are all so; leaving secret judgments to God. To this third opinion I most incline; because we are to judge, that infants of believing parents in their infancy dying are justified, and I find no justification in Scripture without faith. And this hath been the judgment of ancient fathers. Augustine's sermon 14 of the words of the Apostle, *How* (saith he) *do infants believe? By the faith of the parents. If by the faith of parents they be purged, by parent's sin they are polluted. The body of sin in the first parents begot them sinners, and the spirit of life in their latter parents did regenerate them to be believers.* Bernard, epistle 77 saith, *Among the nations as many as were faithful, if they were of years, we believe that they were cleansed by faith and the sacrifices, and that the parent's faith alone availeth for children, yea that it is sufficient for them.* Again, *It is meet and for the honour of God, that to whom age denies their own faith, grace should grant to them a benefit by the faith of an other.*[116]

Thus then it is manifest, that every person must have a faith of his own. Hence we learn, that the doctors of the Romish Church err and are deceived, when they teach, that a man may rest himself in the faith of his teachers, believing in sundry things only as the Church believes, though he knew not distinctly what is the faith of the Church.

---

[116] See further Justin. q. 56. Aug. epist. 23, 57, 105. de bapt. lib.4. cap. 2. Bern. ser. 66 in Cant.

Again, here the Pope's pardons fall to ground. For in vain does the Pope by the power of the keys, apply the meritorious works and the satisfactory sufferings of one man to another, considering every man is saved only by his own faith. The wise virgins professed that they had oil no more than served their own turns. They knew not the popish doctrine, that men might have good works enough for themselves, and an overplus for others. Hilary gathereth hence, *that one man's good works cannot be applied to an other*.[117] Jerome saith, *Every man shall receive a reward for his own works: and that one man's works cannot cover another man's faults in the day of judgment*.[118] The speech of Leo may stop the mouths of all Papists. *Though* (saith he) *the death of the saints be precious in the sight of God, yet the killing of no innocent is the reconciliation of the world. The righteous have received crowns but they have not given crowns. And the fortitude of believers ministers examples of patience, but not gifts of justice. For the deaths of them all were private or particular: neither did any of them by his funeral discharge another man's debt: considering among the sins of men, Christ our Lord is only found in whom all are crucified, dead, and buried, and risen again*. Paul indeed saith to the Corinthians, *that he desired to be bestowed for their souls*:[119] and, *that he suffers all things for the elect*:[120] but this he speaks in respect of his apostical ministry, and not in respect of any works of satisfaction, performed by him in the behalf of others. Again he says, *I bear*

---

117 Upon Matt. 25

118 Ibidem

119 2 Cor. 12:15

120 2 Tim. 2:10

in mine own body the remainders of the sufferings of Christ:[121] but these remainders are the sufferings which every man must bear for himself. For every disciple of Christ, must take up his own cross, and so accomplish the sufferings of the whole mystical body.

Thirdly, by this we learn, not to rely on the gifts, suffrages, and prayers of others: but to seek for a sufficient and lively faith of our own. The foolish virgins that supposed they might have furnished thenselves with sufficient oil of the wise virgins, were utterly disappointed. Therefore the speech of the Papists is to be detested: *namely, that the suffrages of the living, that is, their fastings, prayers, alms, masses, &c. do three ways help the dead, by way of merit of congruity, by way of entreaty, and by way of satisfaction.*[122]

Lastly here we learn that faith and the justice of good conscience must always go together. And for this cause it is not said, that man lives by faith, but the just man. Let all protestants learn and remember this. For it is God's commandment that we should jointly keep faith and good conscience. And it is a common offence to atheists, papists, and worldlings, that such as pretend faith, fail in the righteousness of good conscience. Some it may be, will say, that it shall suffice for them to call upon God when they are dying, and to die by faith. I answer, that we must not only die and be saved, but also live in this world by our faith.

FINIS.

---

121 Col. 1:24

122 Bellar. de indulg. cap 14. pag. 85.

www.ingramcontent.com/pod-product-compliance
Lightning Source LLC
Chambersburg PA
CBHW011552070526
44585CB00023B/2558